Islam Religion

Your Guide to the Truth about Muslim Beliefs, Culture, Customs, and Traditions, Understanding the Quran, and the Sunni / Shia Split & Conflict

Contents

Contents   2
Introduction 4
Chapter 1: An Introduction to Islam   5
What is Islam?   5
Who is Muhammad then? 5
So who is this God that the Muslims worship? 6
What is the Quran? 6
What will you find in the Quran? 7
What do you call the Muslims' place of worship?   7
What is the Ka'ba and what is its significance? 7
Wait, that's it? No statues, no paintings, nothing?   8
The Universe is Muslim.   8
So the goal of Islam is to force everyone to convert?   9
Chapter 2: Getting to Know Allah   10
So how do Muslims explain the existence of the One True God? 10
How strict are Muslims about not making depictions of God? 10
So Muslims believe in Satan?   11
Jinn? As in genies?! 11
So Muslims believe in Angels as well?   12
What does Islam say about free will?   12
Why? 12
And what are these consequences?   13
Hmmm… Can't we just blame it all on Shaitan?   13
If this is the case, then why would Allah create beings who can choose?   13
Were humans given the same offer of the "gift of trust"? Did Allah allow us to choose to be the way we are? 14
Why is there a need for this Fitrah?   14
Do Muslims believe that we were born sinners? 15
Chapter 3: The Fundamental Beliefs of Islam 17
What are the basic beliefs of Islam?   17

Uhh… Wait, aren't we supposed to make our own choices?
What's the point of having free will if God has already
decreed your fate?   18
What are the Five Pillars of Islam?   18
How is supplication (Du'a) performed?   19
Chapter 4: Life in Islam   22
What are the Four Stages of Life according to Islam?   22
According to Islam, how must one live his life?   22
What are the sins in Islam? 23
What does Islam say about forgiveness? 25
So how do you get saved? How do you repent? 25
Is that why Islam punishments are so severe? What about
chopping off the hands of thieves, isn't that a touch too
barbaric?   26
What is Wudu?   31
Do Muslims really perform animal sacrifice?   31
How does a person convert to Islam?   32
What are Sunnis and Shi'as?   32
Are there any food restrictions in the Islam religion?   34
How do Muslims treat women?   34
Why are Muslim men allowed to marry up to four wives?
35
Still, isn't that unfair? Why aren't women allowed to marry
more than one man?   36
What does Islam say about terrorism?   37

Introduction

I want to thank you and congratulate you for downloading my book, Islam Religion: *Your Guide to the Truth about Muslim Beliefs, Culture, Customs, and Traditions, Understanding the Quran, and the Sunni / Shia Split & Conflict*

This book contains facts that will help you understand the essence of Islam and the basic teachings of the faith.

Islam is one of the major religions in the world, but despite the fact that it has penetrated the mainstream and that followers of the faith continue to grow, it remains blanketed in mystery. Currently, there are between 3 to 4 million Muslims residing in the United States. Islam has transformed the lives of many prominent personalities - from artists to activists to politicians. You may not be aware of it but Islam has touched your life positively in more ways than one.

Today, more than ever, it is important to understand what Islam is really about and what its followers stand for. There's so much misunderstanding and prejudice enveloping the Islam religion and Muslims. In fact, even supporters of this faith are guilty of misreading the very heart of Islam.

If all you know about Islam is obtained from the Internet, then chances are you're not receiving proper education about the religion. This is what you'll get in this book, a birds-eye view of the Islam religion that will enable you to see and appreciate it through neutral eyes.

Through these pages, you will learn the basics of Islam belief including Allah, the Four Stages of Life, the Five Pillars of Islam, and important teachings in the Quran. Understand the concepts of Creation, Heaven, Hell, and Judgment through the Islamic perspective. Lastly, catch a glimpse of what life is like within the laws of Islam.

This way, free from external influences, you may decide for yourself what to think and how to feel about the Islam faith.

Thanks again for downloading this book, I hope you enjoy it!

Chapter 1: An Introduction to Islam

What is Islam?
Islam, in the simplest sense, is a monotheistic religion. The Arabic term translates to "surrender one's will to God".

However, this Arabic word has another definition and that is: "to obtain peace in one's soul".

The followers of this faith are called *Muslims*. Contrary to popular opinion, only 20% of of Muslims are Arabs. The rest are comprised of people from various nationalities, races, and cultural backgrounds.

The Islam religion originated in the city of Mecca. It was in the early 7th century, in this West Arabian Peninsula region (the Hijaz) that the faith was born.

As someone striving to understand the Islam faith, it is important for you to understand that Islam is the *only* proper way to refer to the religion. To call it Mohammedanism would be considered offensive to followers of the faith. Why? Because that would imply that they worship Muhammad.

Who is Muhammad then?
Contrary to what some may think, Muhammad (year 573 – 632) is a human being and not considered by Muslim's as a god. He is, instead, a prophet to whom God had entrusted the mission of teaching his people. Muhammad was born in the Quraysh tribe, specifically in the Hashimi clan. In 612, he

received his first auditory message from God and thus, began his life as a prophet. He was forty years old at that time.

The preaching of the word of God did not go without obstacles. Muhammad and his then small band of followers endured a great deal of persecution from those who did not believe. It came to a point where God commanded them to flee the city of Mecca and migrate north to the city of Medina. That was in the year 622 and this marked the beginning of the Muslim calendar. Muhammad and his followers returned to Mecca after several years where they showed forgiveness to those who fought them.

By the time Muhammad passed on at 63 years old, a huge portion of the Arabian Peninsula was practicing the Islam faith. A hundred years after the prophet died, the religion had found its way to Spain, spread to the West, and reached the East.

Muhammad was more than just a preacher. To the Muslims, he is the most excellent example of a human being. Muhammad is to the Muslims what Buddha is to the Buddhists. He's not a god, but a man who has achieved the highest possible spiritual state that a human could achieve and whose example must be emulated. Thus, he is honored but is *not* worshipped.

While he lived, the prophet displayed the virtues of honesty, compassion, mercy, justice, and courage. Muhammad taught his followers to endeavor exclusively for the favor of God and his reward in the afterlife.

So who is this God that the Muslims worship?

Allah is the name Muslims use to refer to the "One True God". And now for the great surprise: Contrary to what most people think, Muslims do *not* worship a different God from Christians and Jews. They worship the exact same God that Abraham and Moses and Jesus did. As stated in the Muslim's Holy Book (the Quran) itself, Allah is the same God who revealed himself to the Jews and the Christians.

Muslims believe that Allah is omnipotent, omniscient, and omnipresent. Everything in this world exists according to his will. He needs no one yet he is needed by all. He never tires and thus, he does not rest. He owns earth and space. No one may intervene without his consent. Nothing in this world is permanent other than him.

Moreover, the Arabic term Allah is the equivalent of the English term God. And thus, even Arabic-speaking Christians and Jews may refer to God as Allah. Hence, it safe to say that Christians, Jews, and most Abrahamic monotheistic religions worship the One True God even though they each worship him in their own different ways.

Really? But there's so much difference between the Christian, Jewish, and Islam concept of the Almighty!

True. For instance, despite all three being Abrahamic systems of belief, both Muslims and Jews deny the Christian idea of the Holy Trinity. The followers of Islam believe that all other religions have mangled the word of God by combining them with ideas made by man.

What is the Quran?

This book written in Arabic it is the principal source of the teachings in Islam. It is in these scriptures where Muslims base their faith and practice.

The Quran is a written version of 23 years' worth of oral teachings by Muhammad. These teachings were conducted in the city of Mecca and the city of Medina from 610-632.

To Muslims, the Quran is considered as the sacred tongue, the direct word of God.

The *Sunnah* is another book which also contains the words of Muhammad although it is more about his deeds and approved traditions and customs.

What will you find in the Quran?

The Quran covers concepts which are concerned with a human being's way of life, from spiritual wisdom and worship to law and rules of transactions. It even contains detailed lessons on suitable human conduct, how to build a just society, and guidelines for a fair economic system. But fundamentally, the Quran focuses on the relationship between God and his creatures. More of the Quran will be discussed in the succeeding chapters.

What do you call the Muslims' place of worship?

Now, before we go any further, it would be best to correct this here and now. Muslims prefer to refer to their house of worship as a Masjid *not* a mosque.

Masjid is an Arabic word that means "a place of prostration." By the entrance of each masjid, you'll find an area to leave your shoes before you enter.

So where did the word mosque come from? It came from the Spanish term for mosquito. Back in the 15th century, when Christians invaded Muslim Spain, the armies of King

Ferdinand and Queen Isabella would vow to whack Islam prayer houses as though they're nothing but mosquitoes. Clearly, it would be best not to use this inappropriate name to refer to Islamic houses of worship.

People who do not follow the Muslim faith are allowed to enter the masjid as long as they are respectful of the building and the people within.

Being Muhammad's birthplace, Mecca is considered by the Muslims as the holy city. In the heart of Mecca, you will find the Great Masjid. Outside this house of worship, you'll see an arcade which consists of a succession of arches circling a courtyard. In the latter, you'll find the Ka'ba, Islam's most sacred shrine.

What is the Ka'ba and what is its significance?

The Ka'ba is a cube-like structure erected around a black stone (meteorite). Followers of the Islam faith believe that this stone came directly from Allah, placed there by Abraham and his son to symbolize their covenant with God. To Muslims, the stone also symbolizes the covenant between Allah and their community. For this reason, when Muslims pray each day for five times, they always do so facing the Ka'ba.

Today, the Ka'ba is 43 feet high although in Muhammad's time, it stood only around 15 ft. Back then, the Ka'ba was filled with hundreds of idols but Muhammad cleansed the building of them. Since then, the structure consists only of a few lamps which symbolize the divine presence of Allah.

Wait, that's it? No statues, no paintings, nothing?

Another important thing that you need to know about the Islam faith is that it expressly forbids the depiction of Allah into any shape or form fashioned by one's imagination. Why? That's because one cannot really draw or carve what he hasn't seen. And if one is to be honest to himself or to others, the first step would be to avoid self-deception by mixing facts with one's imagination.

Nowadays, dozens of televangelists claim to be in contact with God on a regular basis. Believers of the Islam faith are averse to these kinds of claims. No one has ever seen God. Not even Muhammad. According to Islam tradition, the great prophet Moses was the only one who ever came close. But so striking the sight of the Almighty that Moses passed out before he could even catch a glimpse of Allah.

It's for this reason why the literature and arts created in Islamic civilization are devoid of divine imagery.

Islam is not the only religion which prohibits depictions of God but so far it's the only one which has succeeded.

In the next chapter, you'll learn more about how the Muslims perceive Allah.

The Universe is Muslim.
Come again?

Look at the shared letters SLM in Islam and in Muslim. In Arabic, this root word roughly translates to "to entrust one's whole being to another".

What most people don't know is that the word Muslim is not only used for people but also for anything and everything which surrenders itself to the will of Allah.

Take a look at nature and space: the water, the rocks, the planets, molecules and atoms... They all exist and function in accordance with the natural laws which Allah had created. Look at the world around you and you'll see that everything is doing precisely what it's meant to do. Everything is precisely as it's meant to be. Plainly put, everything around you is surrendered to God's will. *Everything is Muslim.*

All of creation, no matter how big or small, each praises Allah in its own way. The river runs and so do the beasts, the birds sing and the frogs croak their wet serenade, the trees dance to the rhythm of the wind... All these things they do out of sheer joy of *being*.

When you see this, you'll realize that even *you* must surrender to the will of Allah. It is the only way to achieve peace. To seek any other way of life would be to go the wrong way.

Simply put, you are either following the way of God or you're going astray. You're either Muslim, or you're going against your very nature, what you are meant to do, and who you are meant to be.

So the goal of Islam is to force everyone to convert?

Not at all. In fact, the Quran specifically states that no person should be coerced into converting to Islam. It is stated in the Quran that there is no sense in coercing anyone into the Muslim way of life because honest belief is valued over forced faith. Furthermore, anyone who has truthfully embraced Allah and rejects committing transgression has already fastened himself securely to God.

Chapter 2: Getting to Know Allah

So how do Muslims explain the existence of the One True God?

According to believers in the Islam faith, the existence of Allah can be explained through these four facts:

The wondrous beauty and intricacy of the natural world reveals the intelligence behind the creation of the universe. In other words, a designing mind must have made it all.

Human beings have the possession of moral choice and physical, mental, and emotional abilities and capacities that are beyond those of plants and animals. Therefore, someone must have given these things to us.

The presence of God is made clearer by the holy guidance received by Muhammad and other prophets. Also, there's the fact that we receive flashes of insight on a personal level thus, proving that a higher power is guiding us.

Another proof is our internal emotions which drive us to search for the meaning of things. Our souls are constantly seeking to be in harmony with nature and with higher powers in the universe. In the end, everything's so simple: Why would human beings ask *why* in the first place if there is no *because*? The truth is we ask questions because answers exist.

How strict are Muslims about not making depictions of God?

Very. Apart from children's toys, Muslims are not allowed to fashion realistic depictions of people and beasts.

The huge difference between Islam and most religions is that it is not easily influenced by the changing times. Islam abhors Western pop culture's depiction of God as a kindly old man or an innocent child or even as a juvenile psychopath. To Muslims, these are pure blasphemy.

You'll understand now that the reason why Muslims opt not to watch even kid's films which portray God or Jesus or Moses is not because they are against God or Jesus or Moses or any other prophet. Instead, it's because they believe that to represent them without having first-hand knowledge of them is wrong and disrespectful.

Another thing that Muslims find most appalling is how people these days promote the idea that God is within each of us and that we can somehow tap into his divine powers. People these days are fond of using and abusing the phrase *God is Love* just so it could make all sorts of behavior acceptable. If one wants to commit sin, they do it because hey, *God is Love*! And so more and more, people use these three words to deviate from the original teachings of God just to suit their own desires.

According to the Quran, Allah did not send anyone any authority to make up names or depictions of God. Everything done based on pure conjecture is blasphemy and idolatry for they are nothing but reflections of your soul's desire.

The Quran also warned believers that the desire of Satan is to separate man from God. So what does Satan do? He appeals to the desire of our souls. And of course, the cleverest way to divide man from God is by letting man think that he/she is a god/goddess in his/her own right.

So Muslims believe in Satan?
Followers of the Islam faith acknowledge the existence of Shaitan though not as the epitome of ultimate evil. Who is Shaitan then? Shaitan roughly translates to "to pull away from". And that is exactly what Shaitan does, pull us away from God.

Shaitain is anything and anyone who goes against the will of Allah. So, in a way, it's possible for a person to be Shaitan.

In other dimensions exist beings known as *Jinn*. They are the creatures who refuse to submit themselves to the will of Allah.

Jinn? As in genies?!
Not as portrayed in the Disney films. As awesome as it may seem, jinns don't live in magic lamps and vintage rings.

Jinn are life forms which are made up of an undetectable substance and exist for no other purpose other than their own. Contrary to what the Hollywood movies show, humans cannot control them. However, *they* can manipulate *us*.

Believers of the Islam faith do not believe in ghosts and such. But according to them, jinns are the sources of paranormal phenomena. Jinns are capable of manifesting themselves to humans and delivering false messages so as to keep them farther away from Allah. A jinn can goad you into committing sin. So while some preachers or psychics might think that it's God who's talking to them, it could very well be just a jinn trying to mislead them and the people around them.

Modern Muslim scholars hold the theory that jinns dwell in the realm of energy wave spectrums. It's for this reason why they can communicate with us through our thoughts by altering our brain waves.

Unlike humans, jinns already know for certain that God exists and yet they choose not to follow him.

Angels, on the other hand, are intrinsically good beings. They were created Muslim and thus, cannot fall from grace as the Christian tradition suggests.

So Muslims believe in Angels as well?

Angels are beings created by Allah way before the creation of man. They are made up of light energy but they have the power to transform into anything to fit into the physical realm. Angels are neither male not female. They are creatures of intelligence but unlike us, they are devoid of free will and emotional imperfections.

The following are the four main angels in Islam:

Jibra'il who's also known as Gabriel. Jibra'il is Allah's messenger to prophets. Gabriel is the one who gave Muhammed his first auditory revelation.

Mika'il is the one responsible for controlling the weather.

Azra'il is known as the Angel of Death.

And Israfil is the angel tasked to blow the horn when the world ends.

Just as jinns are meant to deceive us and lead us astray, angels are meant to look over us and provide us with useful insight in our daily struggles.

What does Islam say about free will?

According to the Quran, long before the creation of man, Allah spoke with everything in the universe to offer them the gifts of self-awareness and free will. These gifts are referred to as "the trust". And if they choose to receive the gift of trust, they would be able to transcend nature.

But as it is, the angels, the beasts, the mountains, and the stars chose not to take the gift. They were content with surrendering themselves utterly to Allah.

Why?

Because this gift comes with a responsibility. A beast may not be blamed from stealing food from another animal. Such is its nature. But when a man steals from another, it's a completely different thing because humans are capable of distinguishing good from evil. We are capable of choosing between right and wrong.

To put things plainly, the rest of the universe said no to this gift because they feared the consequences.

And what are these consequences?

Believers of the Islam faith believe in Hell. If you reject God and allow your soul to be corrupted by leading a life of meaningless pleasure, then you'll end up in hell. However, contrary to the Christian concept of eternal damnation, you won't stay in hell forever.

The purpose of hell is to cleanse your soul in fire so that it may be able to reunite itself with Allah. Once your soul has been cleansed, you will be rewarded in heaven for the good deeds that you have done while you lived.

That said, there are some souls that are too completely corrupted that they end up remaining in hell. But then again,

Islam teaches us that it is Allah alone who understands the secrets of one's heart. He knows its intentions far better than one knows himself. Trust that God will reward and punish people justly.

Hmmm... Can't we just blame it all on Shaitan?

Absolutely not. The Quran is very clear about our accountability as human beings. No matter how we were tempted or misled, in the end, we were the ones who decided and carried out our actions.

We possess reason and free will. We are urged to use them.

Muslims believe that when you die, you face Allah alone. And when this happens, you cannot blame others or even Shaitan for how you chose to live out your life.

According to the Quran, when Judgment comes, Shaitan will admit that it was Allah who gave you the True Promise of salvation and not he. He will say that you cannot blame him, only yourself. Then, he will reject how you associated him with God. Furthermore, he will agree that you must pay the price of your sins in hell.

If this is the case, then why would Allah create beings who can choose?

Indeed, why create jinns who then ended up refusing to follow him?

What's the point of giving humans free will when everything else in the world is Muslim (already surrendered to his will)?

To answer this, contemplate on this question: Of what use is treasure if it is buried?

Allah *wanted to be known*. He wanted to be discovered. He wanted us to find our way to him. If there are dire consequences for straying from the path of God, there are also unimaginably glorious rewards for walking straight in his path. Allah wants us to reap those rewards.

And what is this ultimate prize: Love and fellowship with him.

According to Islam, a man achieves completeness and ultimate peace when he is one with the will of God. The closer you get to him, the more content you will become.

Allah said that he created the universe for himself and for us. There is so much beauty in being created human. Whatever words Allah whispered to the flower to make it bloom, he whispered those words into your heart and made it a hundred times more beautiful.

Were humans given the same offer of the "gift of trust"? Did Allah allow us to choose to be the way we are?

Being a just God, he did. Before, we weren't as we are now. Humans were just a muddy prototype mingled in a kind of embryonic soup-like spirit matter. Imagine a gigantic ball made up of compressed souls. None of these souls were special or unique.

When Allah offered the gift of trust, the spirit collective took it. And from this mutual mass of souls, each individual human would later get its own soul. (the *Ruh*)

And so human beings were made flesh. They roamed the earth possessing reason and self-awareness and free will. Humans are guided by a moral compass known as the *Fitrah*. This is your natural inclination which guides you as you navigate through life.

According to the Quran, when you were still in the womb, an angel provided you with a *ruh* (soul) along with an in-built fitrah.

Why is there a need for this Fitrah?

It is the fitrah which nudges us to the right direction. To understand it better, think of the small voice in your head saying "No, this is wrong". Think of the emotion you feel when you witness someone doing an utterly selfless act. For each time you think twice before you sin, for each time you feel *touched* because someone did something nice, that's your fitrah at work.

This Fitrah is our weapon against Shaitan who is ever pulling us away from Allah.

Each human has an animal within. All of us desire pleasure in various forms and we all seek satisfaction for our animal urges. Reason is not enough to help us stay in the right path when, like animals, we are all instinctively inclined to procreate, store more food and wealth than we need, and seek creature comforts.

Come to think of it, if people in this world focused more on things that truly mattered, instead of on wealth and worldly comforts, then the world could be a better place. Take global warming as an example. The science and technology is available. The problem can be solved. But how come nothing is being done about it? That's because humans today have their priorities all twisted. And it's for this reason why Islam frowns upon the wasteful and meaningless manner in which people live their lives today.

Islam frowns upon a life of excess and attachment to worldly things. After all, you can bring none of these things to the afterlife.

In Islam, there is the gravest sin called *Shirk*. It means holding in your heart something equal to Allah. To hold anything or anyone in your heart dearer than you hold God is forbidden. Vanity and boastfulness are minor forms of shirk. When you do this, it's as though you are competing with Allah himself. The Quran urges us to remember that when we die, we shall all return to dust. Everything that we possess and know right now, we owe to Allah. So instead of showing off our endowments and earthly accomplishments, we should spend more time expressing our gratitude to God instead.

In the next chapter, you'll learn more about which deeds are considered as sins in Islam.

Do Muslims believe that we were born sinners?

No. As you might've noticed, except for the important points previously mentioned, the story of the Creation in Islam tradition is not much different from the Judeo-Christian tradition. Here is another huge difference: According to Muslims, when Adam sinned against God, God forgave him.

The prophet Muhammad said that all children were birthed with the natural inclination to be Muslim, to submit themselves to the will of Allah. However, his parents or his environment might fashion him into something else that's so far divorced from his true nature. An example is when a child's parent decides to turn him into a Christian, or a Jew, or even an atheist. But with one's fitrah, hopefully, he shall find his way back to Allah.

The message of Islam is simple: Stop fighting God's will. Embrace your true nature. Join the rest of the universe in worshipping and loving him. Only then will you find true tranquility and happiness.

What does Islam say about Jesus?

It is important to note that the whole construction of Christianity is founded on the assumption that we were all born tainted with the original sin. Thus, it was necessary for God to send us his son so that he may take away those sins.

Islam does not deny the existence of Jesus. Neither does it refute his virgin birth. In truth, Islam looks upon Jesus as a prophet of God and his birth as an amazing miracle by Allah. That said, Muslims don't take it as a sign that he's a god or that he's a part of God or the son of God. Allah did not have to send his son down to us because there was *no original sin* to begin with.

An Islamic term called *Tauhid* means "indivisible oneness". It suggests that Allah is one and solitary in his divinity. As the Quran says: If there is more than one god, then each god would have laid claim and lorded over what he had created.

The beauty of Islam is that it tells us that our ultimate fate isn't doomed by something that happened ages ago, through an act which we didn't even take part of. Instead, the fate of our soul lies entirely on what *we* choose to do right now, in this lifetime, at this very moment.

Chapter 3: The Fundamental Beliefs of Islam

What are the basic beliefs of Islam?

The following are the six basic beliefs of Islam. If one is to be a true Muslim, he must believe *all* six.

- **There is only one God and he is singular and incomparable.**

You must call upon no other. You must pray to no other.

To say that we have been created out of his image and likeness would be to besmirch his name.

- **Angels exist and are to be honored.**

Angels worship and obey Allah. They act out his will.

- **Allah provided his messengers with revelations through his books.**

The purpose of the Quran is to provide guidance for mankind.

God's word in the Quran must be protected from any kind of corruption or alteration which will lead to its misinterpretation.

- **God has prophets.**

Some of these prophets include Adam, Abraham, Moses, Noah, and Jesus.

They all serve as his messengers and yet none of them possess the divine qualities of God.

However, Allah's last message was revealed to no other than Muhammad. To put it plainly, Muhammad is considered as the last prophet.

- **In the Day of Judgment, everyone will be resurrected so that they may be judged by Allah.**

All will be judged according to what they believed in and what they had done.

A person who dies believing in gods other than Allah and following the teachings of prophets other than Muhammad, will lose his place in Paradise. Simply put, you have to be Muslim in order to be accepted in heaven.

Moreover, Muslims believe that life in the Hereafter is greatly similar to life as you know it now. You'll have your spirit as well as your physical body. The difference is that life in the hereafter is a whole lot longer than life here on earth. Imagine a drop of water versus an ocean.

- **The Al-Qadar**

The Divine Predestination states that Allah is the creator of all things. Whatever Allah wills, it occurs. Whatever Allah wills not to transpire, does not occur.

In short, nothing will happen to you except for what has God decreed for you.

Uhh... Wait, aren't we supposed to make our own choices? What's the point of having free will if God has already decreed your fate?

Make no mistake, with your decisions, your beliefs and your actions, it is still up to you whether you end up in heaven or in hell.

But Allah is all-knowing. Unlike you or me, he is not limited by the boundaries of space and time. He knows everything that has transpired and all that which will transpire.

Allah records everything that transpires and that which will transpire.

Simply put, he knows what decision you will make even before you make it. He knows whether you will end up in heaven or in hell even before you pass on to the afterlife.

What are the Five Pillars of Islam?

- **The Shahadah**

The Shahadah is a sentence said at least said 17 times a day in the prayers of a Muslim. It is a statement declaring allegiance to Allah. Translated to English, it goes: "I declare that there is no true deity other than Allah and that Muhammad is a true messenger of God." In these two phrases, you'll find the two founding principles of Muslim faith.

By saying this several times a day, you are constantly reminding yourself of God's presence in your life. This is good especially in these days when it's easy enough to lose ourselves in the hustle and bustle of daily living.

By continually reminding yourself of your commitment to God, you are enabling yourself to focus emotionally and mentally on your ultimate purpose in life. That is, to surrender to God's will and to lead a virtuous existence by following the example of Muhammad.

- **The Salat**

This pillar refers to the daily ritual prayers. Muslims recite five prayers each day and each one takes only a few minutes. These are done at dawn (Fajr), after noontime (Zuhr), during the afternoon ('Asr), after the sun sets (Maghrib), and at night ('Isha).

When one prays, he feels an internal sense of peace, joy, and comfort. Muhammad himself instructed his followers to pray so that they may be comforted by the act.

Prayer is considered as your direct link to Allah. You pray by your own without the need for intermediaries.

That said, Salat is not to be mistaken for personal prayers or supplications (Du'a) to Allah. While the latter is optional, Salat is something that a Muslim must do as his daily duty.

Praying is allowed almost everywhere from workplaces to open fields.

How is supplication (Du'a) performed?
When a Muslim makes a personal request to God, he holds his hands out in front of him, both palms facing skyward. By

doing this, he is asking to receive God's blessing. Then, he communicates his request to Allah. After that, he passes his palms over his face. By doing this, he is washing Allah's grace over his face.

- **Zakat**

This is the third pillar which refers to the yearly charity which followers of the Islam faith take part of. The term translates to *purification* but it also means *growth*. And these two are exactly what you achieve when you give. By setting aside a percentage of your wealth for the needy, you are purifying your wealth. You could liken it to trimming garden bushes. By performing Zakat, you are promoting proper personal growth and at the same time supporting equilibrium in the allocation of resources.

Muslims believe that everything belongs to God and that includes any material goods that one possesses. Whatever wealth you own, Allah had merely entrusted to you. You may also give as much as you please for voluntary charity.

- **Saum**

This fourth pillar of faith is the annual fasting at the month of Ramadan (9th month of Islamic calendar). Followers of the Islam religion fast beginning from dawn to sunset.

They abstain not only from food and drink but also from sexual activities.

This is done for the purpose of spiritual purification.

How does it work?

By severing your ties to earthly comforts, even momentarily, you enable yourself to develop empathy to those who truly hunger and thirst.

This is also the time to fortify family ties and make peace with people who have done you wrong. Simply put, this is the season to cleanse your thoughts, your emotions, and your life.

- **Hajj**

This fifth pillar refers to the pilgrimage to Mecca which is considered as a once in a lifetime duty. Not everyone may be economically and physically capable of joining this pilgrimage but those who are, they are urged to do this.

The yearly pilgrimage is done in the 12th month of the Islam calendar. Male and female pilgrims wear Ahram clothing. These simple garments are donned so that each pilgrim, regardless of social status, are equals when put before the presence of Allah. In a way, the Hajj enables you to catch a glimpse of the Judgment day.

Approximately a couple of million people visit Mecca each year from various corners of the earth.

What do pilgrims do there?

They ask God for forgiveness and also communicate to him their personal appeals.

This is also the time to reevaluate how you've been spending your life.

The end of this pilgrimage is marked by Eid al-Fitr, a celebration which commemorates the culmination of Ramadan and Eid Al-Adha, a holiday with is celebrated through prayer.

Why is Friday considered the special day of worship for Muslims?

Muslims pray every day. But once a week, the men are required to pray as a congregation. Friday is considered to be a significant day because it was the day when Adam, the first man, was created. It was also the day that he committed sin after being tempted by Shaitan. Thus, it was the day when Adam was banished from Paradise. Moreover, Friday is when the Day of Judgment will occur.

Chapter 4: Life in Islam

What are the Four Stages of Life according to Islam?

In the previous chapter, we talked about the creation of man from that primordial ball of collective souls. The thing is that those souls, like everything else in this world, belong to God. To put things simply, your soul is not your own. It is merely lent to you by Allah.

According to Islam, we have to pass through four stages to find our way back to the Creator.

These stages are:

Your time in your mother's womb

Your time in the physical realm

Your time in the grave

Your time in the afterlife, either in heaven or in hell

According to Islam, how must one live his life?

To surrender oneself to Allah does not only mean believing in him but also to lead a lifestyle that advocates harmony among human beings and all of creation. This means that you have to follow a personal morality code.

The revelations of God served to show people the right path throughout history, from the Gospels, to the Torah, to the Songs of David, etc. Contrary to what some might think, Islam does not deny their validity at all.

However, the Quran does state that God's earlier revelations have all failed to survive without being tampered with by the human hand.

These are the righteous deeds that are encouraged in Muslims:

One must always speak the truth.

One must treat family members with kindness.

One should honor his parents.

One must give to charity.

One must make it his obligation to feed the less-privileged.

One has the duty to battle against injustice.

One must free those who are enslaved.

One must always return any property that was borrowed.

One has the duty to study and to learn.

One has the responsibility to be kind to other creatures.

What are the sins in Islam?

Islam does not have a list of commandments but the Quran mentioned more than a hundred sins to avoid. Based from the teachings of Muhammad, all followers of the Islam faith are warned not to do the following sins:

Committing adultery by worshipping other gods or associating persons or objects with Allah.

Taking another person's life.

Not performing prayer.

- Not participating in Zakat.
- Failing to fast during Ramadan. (unless one has a valid excuse ex. health conditions)
- Failing to perform Hajj when one has the health and the resources to do so.
- Bringing dishonor to one's parents and shunning relatives.
- Committing adultery.
- Engaging in sodomy.
- Exploiting others through business and gaining wealth through illegal means. This also includes collecting interest.
- Telling lies about God and his messengers.
- Deceiving one's followers and being unjust. (Applicable to those in leadership positions)
- Displaying arrogance and pride.
- Intoxication with alcohol and other harmful substances.
- Lying, bearing false testimony against others, and taking false oath.
- Engaging in gambling.
- Slandering innocent women.
- Committing theft in any way.
- Oppressing others in any way.
- Taking one's own life.
- Judging others unfairly.
- Stealing from and mistreating orphans.

Participating in bribery, whether you offer it or receive it.

Females imitating males and vice versa.

Performing deceptions through any form.

Marrying a woman who was divorced.

Bearing the knowledge of Islam religion and the word of Allah and keeping it only to oneself.

Betraying those who have trusted in you.

Boasting about one's good deeds.

Gossiping and eavesdropping to other people's discussions.

Cursing and blaspheming.

Breaking one's word or breech of written agreements.

Placing one's faith in fortune tellers and psychics.

Dabbling with magic.

Being disrespectful to one's husband and being overbearing to one's wife.

Performing any form of offensive act or speech against others.

Carrying out disputes with violence.

Forming evil deeds *and* intentions.

What does the Quran say about committing these sins?

When a person commits any of the sins mentioned above, it will be held against him on the Day of Judgment.

As previously mentioned, Allah records all that transpires. According to the prophet Muhammad, when a person has good intentions, it is written down as a good deed. However, when a person has a good intention and follows through with good action, it is written down as a thousand good deeds.

If a person is tempted to do a bad deed but does not act on it, God writes it down as a good deed.

However, if a person develops a bad intention and acts on it, it will be written down as one bad deed. Even so, the implication of this one bad deed is not to be taken lightly for surely, the sinner shall pay a heavy price for it on Judgment Day.

What does Islam say about forgiveness?

Unlike in other religions, followers of the Islam faith do not require another person to serve as an intercessor between him and God.

When asking for forgiveness, there are no go-betweens for when you face the Creator, there shall be no mediators.

This is another great thing about the Islam faith. It greatly emphasizes the human being's accountability for his deeds.

As you can see now, Islam is a religion that promotes the use of intelligence and free will. It is up to you to do what's right or wrong. And it is up to you to suffer the consequences.

You will not be tainted by a sin committed by someone else. (ex. the original sin) Likewise, no one else will die for you to deliver you from your sins.

Furthermore, no one else will ask forgiveness for you. No one else will make amends for your wrongdoings. No one else, not even demons, shall be blamed for them.

There's only you and your reason and your free will and your fitrah. Whether you will be saved or damned is completely up to you.

So how do you get saved? How do you repent?

In order to erase the stain of your evil deeds, you need to perform Tawba which is a process of repentance involving four steps:

First, you must feel genuine remorse about the evil deed.

Second, you must expressly ask Allah to forgive you.

Third, you must make amends for the sin as much as possible.

And fourth, you must resolve never to perform the evil act again.

Do all these and Allah will forgive you.

However, these steps alone apply to the personal moral sins that one commits.

There are some evil deeds which bring harm to others. If such is the case, to be forgiven, you must pay the price for these sins not just in the afterlife but also *in this life*. Such sins involve social crimes like murder and stealing.

The thing about Islamic law is that it combines civil and criminal law with individual morality to form a singular general code. This is in adherence with the religious belief that there exists no dissimilarity between the earthly realm and the spiritual realm.

To state things plainly, the phrase *God forgives* may not be used as an excuse for a sinner to get off lightly.

That said, only criminal activities and not personal moral sins may be put on trial in the presence of a judge.

Is that why Islam punishments are so severe? What about chopping off the hands of thieves, isn't that a touch too barbaric?

Yes, there is a verse in the Quran that states plainly that one may cut a thief's hands. Even so, it also states that should the thief repent and amend his behavior, then Allah will forgive him for he is a merciful God.

Note that the cutting hands part is just one verse in the Quran. Thirty-nine other verses emphasize that should the sinner repent, Allah will forgive him. And if Allah can forgive, how can you, a mere human being, not?

Moreover, the Quran continuously begs and reminds the reader to provide punishments that are in proportion to the crime.

According to one verse in the Quran, if a person decides to forgive the sinner and reconciles, he shall reap rewards from Allah. Even in the case of murder, this verse provides the aggrieved party (the family of the deceased) with the option to spare the sinner's life especially if the killing was accidental.

In most forms of crimes, the victims and the families of the victims have the option to receive compensation from the guilty party as they see fit. In other words, the victim or the family of the victim has the right to fix the amount of punishment or compensation for the sin committed against them.

Thus, the act of "cutting" may be interpreted into various ways:

The physical cutting of the criminal's hands

The cutting of flesh/ the marking of the criminal's hands

Cutting the criminal's power to repeat the crime (ex. imprisonment)

Cutting the criminal's sustenance (ex. providing compensation)

But here's another thing that's often overlooked by those who read the Quran: More than expressing the need to carry out just punishment, the Quran repeatedly urges us to pursue a better path. That path is the path of forgiveness.

An eye for an eye, sure. But according to the Quran, if you withdraw from retaliating, it will be considered as an act of atonement for yourself.

Additionally, if the injured person fails to judge correctly and if he delivers a punishment that's harsher than Allah had revealed, then that person will be considered as no better than the evil-doer. Remember, Allah is watching and is keeping a record of it all.

Chapter 5: Basic Islamic Customs and Traditions

One of the most common customs of Muslims is to pronounce the name of Allah before partaking in food or drink.

The purpose of this is to recognize God's manifold blessings. Another is to express your request for Allah to continue blessing you with abundance. According to Muhammad: Each time someone eats, he is supposed to say: "I begin with the name of Allah."

Let's say you're very hungry then you forgot to pray, what then?

Then say these words: "With the name of Allah, at the beginning and at the end."

Another common Islamic custom is to use your right hand when you eat or drink.

Allah ordered us to use his prophets as an example. Muhammad was a very hygiene-conscious person who encouraged his followers to perform clean acts with the right hand (eating, shaking hands, writing, etc.) and to perform dirty acts with the left hand (washing oneself in the toilet etc.)

Note that back in an era where people ate with their bare hands, such sanitary practices were vital. Even today where people use forks and knives when dining, this practice is retained in the Islam culture.

So if you're a lefty, don't worry, you will not go to hell for it.

Muslims must greet brothers properly by saying "Assalaam 'alaikum" upon meeting.

Meanwhile, when greeted by someone this way, one should respond by saying: "Wa 'alaikum Assalaam".

By doing so, you are expressing your desire for peace and offering your supplication of blessings for the recipient.

According to Muhammad, the young must greet the elders first before the younger ones. Furthermore, the passerby must first greet the person who is seated before those who are standing. Also, a smaller group must be the first one to greet a bigger group.

According to Islam tradition, sneezing is considered as a relief from a fleeting bodily disorder. Thus, after one sneezes, he should thank Allah by saying the following: "Al-Hamdulillah."

At the same time, those people who have witnessed this must also pray for mercy and blessings for the person who has thanked Allah. They are supposed to say: "Yarhamukallah." In English, it crudely translates to: "Bless you!"

In return, the person who sneezed and thanked God must again respond with something akin to: "May Allah guide you in leading a more virtuous life."

This whole exchange is referred to as *Tashmeet*.

Another popular custom of the Muslims is to recite Adhaan to the newborn's right ear and the Iqaamah to the child's left ear. The former term translates to "call for prayer". According to Muhammad, this message contains the abridged message of Islam. It is a call for total surrender to the will of God.

All Muslims are continuously called towards the Adhaan's message. As such, the Adhaan is pronounced in the masjid every single day for five times.

Repeat "God is the greatest." for four times.

Twice, testify to the fact that there is no other deity except for God.

Twice, testify to the fact that Muhammad is God's messenger.

For two times, say "Come fast to prayer."

For two times, say "Come fast to success."

Once again, say "God is the greatest." two times.

Then say this once: "There is no other god but God."

Muslims are also particular about the habit of cleansing the body.

Muhammad encouraged his followers to trim their facial hair as well as their pubic hair, even those under the armpits. He instructed them to cut their nails short. Circumcision is also an Islamic custom performed to the male children.

According to the prophet, wearing unkempt and large beards are a sign of self-importance. Allah frowns upon this. Additionally, there's the issue of cleanliness since such facial hair can contaminate food. According to Muslim tradition, it would be wrong to leave facial or pubic hair unshaven or fingernails unclipped for a duration of forty days.

According to the teachings, we must keep our appearances clean to honor the fact that we were created separately from beasts.

Another important religious tradition is to maintain the cleanliness of the nose, the mouth, and the teeth. Muhammad himself rinsed his mouth and nose when he washed.

Muhammad was reported to have said that if it would not have been too burdensome for his followers, he would have instructed them to brush their teeth prior to praying.

Muslims are also very strict about Istinjaa. This refers to cleansing organs involved with urination and elimination. Depending on the situation, this washing may be done with water or with dry earth. (when water is scarce)

According to the Quran, in order to keep Allah's love, one must continually keep both one's soul and one's body clean.

Another common Muslim practice is to refrain from having sexual relations with a woman who is menstruating. Couples must also abstain when the woman is having her puerperal discharge. The Quran states that a man may make love to his wife *after* she has cleansed herself (when her period is over).

Furthermore, the Quran clarified that this does not mean that a woman is considered *dirty* when she's having her period. Nor must she be treated as an untouchable.

Additionally, couples must also bathe after sexual contact.

One is to follow this order:

Wash the hands.

Cleanse the sexual organ with your left hand.

Rinse the head and the hair.

Bathe the feet.

As previously mentioned, our bodies are not our own. They are the property of Allah. Thus, it is our duty to take care of this borrowed vessel for the soul.

What is Wudu?

Wudu is a purification ritual which Muslims must perform before participating in prayers. To do this, one must cleanse carefully his hands, his face, his arms, and his feet. Because Muslims pray five times a day, this means they have to perform these ablutions five times daily as well.

Do Muslims really perform animal sacrifice?

It may seem odd and primitive and even surprising considering that the Islam faith does not condone the hurting and senseless killing of animals. However, note that the meat of these animals do not go to waste since they are used for sustenance.

Remember, everything in this world belongs to Allah. When Muslims kill an animal for food, they mention the name of Allah. In a way, they are asking for God's permission to kill the animal for their benefit. In occasions when the sacrificial animal's meat is not to be consumed, it is to be given to the poor.

Chapter 6: More Must Knows About Islam

How does a person convert to Islam?
Converting to Islam is surprisingly easy. You merely have to say the Shahada.

That said, you must utter the words with conviction and understand their full meaning.

Really, it's that easy. The challenge comes not in the conversion but in how you actually follow the Islam way of life.

Remember also that as a Muslim, you have to have faith in the Quran and take it as the literal word of Allah.

What are Sunnis and Shi'as?
Like most major religions, Islam has spawned various sects. However, the most widely known are Sunni and Shi'a. These two sects are rooted way back in the infanthood of the Islamic caliphate (Islamic state). To understand things more clearly, think of the division between the Catholic and the Protestants. That said, the schism did not occur due to disagreements in the doctrine. Instead, it began with the differences in the preferences for the caliph (Islam's political and religious leader).

In the year 632, after the death of Muhammad, Abu Bakr was elected as the first caliph. However, Muhammad's cousin, Ali, initially refused to support the new caliph. He and his supporters argued that he should've been provided with an equal chance in being elected as the caliph.

In the end, Ali and his supporters swore allegiance to the new leader but unavoidably, there was bad blood between them. After Abu Bakr's rule, new caliphs were elected and Ali's supporters watched angrily from the sidelines as their chosen leader was continuously ignored.

In 656, Ali was finally chosen as caliph. However, his triumph was short-lived as the clan of Bany Umayyah took over.

And thus began the formation of the Shi'a sect by Ali's supporters. They fought back and in 680 AD, Muhammad's grandson, Hussain with his 72 companions, battled against the massive army of Yazid (the existing caliphate).

Hussain died but he lived such an exceptional life of honor and integrity that his followers hailed him as a martyr.

Generally, a Muslim who is not part of the Shi'a sect is referred to as Sunni. You should also know that most of the teachings in this book reflect the teachings from the Sunni sect of Islam.

The following are the main differences between the two Islamic sects:

Currently, the Shi'a sect have approximately 200 million followers. Meanwhile, the Sunni sect have about 1.2 billion followers.

The Shi'a sect believed that the prophet Muhammad himself had meant for his cousin Ali to become his successor. The Sunni sect disagrees, believing that other men have the equal right to be nominated and elected for the position.

According to the Shi'a sect, their ruler must be male children from Ali's lineage. (Ali was married to Muhammad's daughter Fatima.) On the other hand, the Sunnis do not approve of dynasties. According to them, any practicing Muslim may be selected for the position.

To the Shi'ites, an Imam (prayer leader) is the *only* one allowed to interpret the Quran. They also believe that Allah provides Imams with revelations. The Sunnis think otherwise. They believe that the Imams are to be regarded as saintly persons with sturdy faith in the Quran. However, they believe that Muhammad was the last man to receive commandments from Allah.

The term Shi'a translates to "partisans", as in, members of the party of Ali. The word Sunni translates to "tradition."

In the first month of the Islamic calendar (Muharram), the Shi'a memorialize Hussain's martyrdom. They gather to march in parades on the tenth day of Muharram and some would perform self-flagellation. That is, they would beat their own backs with chains or blades. The Sunni sect abhors this practice. They look at it as a violation to one's body (which is the property of Allah) and consider it as a major sin.

The Shi'a permit their followers to build and visit shrines. They are also allowed to worship graves. Conversely, the Sunnis consider these as Shirk and blasphemies.

According to the Shi'ites, angels possess a limited amount of free will and are not above sin. The Sunnis, on the other hand, view angels as beings with no free will and are completely surrendered to Allah's will.

The clergy of the Shi'ites include the Imam, the Ayatollah (prestigious title for clergymen), the Mujtahid (original authority in the Muslim law), the Allamah (honorary title for scholars of Islamic philosophy), the Maulana (respected religious scholars), Hujjat-al Islam (honorific title for scholars below Ayatollah), and Sayyid (males acknowledged as descendants of Muhammad).

The clergy of the Sunni sect includes the Caliph, the Imam, the Mujtahid, the Allamah, and the Maulana.

The original languages of the Shi'a sect includes Farsi and Arabic. The language of the Sunni sect is Arabic.

Important places associated with the Shi'a are Karbala and Kufa. Meanwhile, Mecca and Medina hold special meanings to Sunnis.

When it comes to mandatory alms, 20% of a Shi'ites possessions are to be given to the Imam and to the poor. Meanwhile, a Sunni is expected to give 2.5% of what his has to the needy through Zakat.

While temporary unannounced marriage is allowed by the Shi'a sect, the Sunni sect looks upon it as adultery.

Are there any food restrictions in the Islam religion?

According to the Quran, one is forbidden to eat pork, animals that have been killed as a sacrifice for anyone other than God, carrion flesh, meat from pets, blood, intoxicating substances including alcohol, animals that have died a violent death/slaughtered (ex. strangulation, killed through a blow or from a fall), and animals that have been gored or attacked by a beast of prey. An exception to the latter are animals that have been mercifully killed before it perishes.

In Arabic, the term religion translates to *deen*, which means "way of life". This means that to Muslims, Islam is more than just a philosophy. It is a way of life. And part of being Muslim or surrendering to the will of Allah, is trusting him about what is and isn't good for our bodies, including what we should and shouldn't eat. After all, who would know his creation better than he who created it?

How do Muslims treat women?

Somehow, there is this prejudiced idea that women in Islam are to be considered as second-class citizens. That could not be farther from the truth. Muhammad himself said that women are the other halves of men. This means a man is not complete without a woman and vice versa. Contrary to what some might believe, Islam is a religion which strives to empower women.

Islamic laws include the following:

The property of a woman may not be taken by a man, not even her husband.

Women shall not be deprived of their right to be educated.

To ruin an innocent woman's reputation is considered as a criminal act.

It is the right of women to file legal suits in court. They are allowed to give sole testimony.

Women are allowed to ask for a divorce.

By default, women are granted custody of small children after divorce.

Alimony and palimony are obligatory.

Women may freely engage into contracts.

Domestic abuse is punishable by law.

In the workplace, women must get equal wages.

Women are allowed to vote and even run for office.

No woman is to be coerced into entering into marriage.

In cases of arranged marriages, both men and women are allowed to break off the engagement.

There's a story where a girl came to Muhammad seeking help because she was forced into marriage. The prophet immediately had the wedding annulled.

It is important to understand that pre-Islamic Arabia did not have any laws to protect women and children. As a result, they suffered greatly. Women were treated as property. They were sold like cattle. Female infants were considered useless and helpless and thus, parents would bury them alive. Understand that in times when war was frequent and poverty widespread, people believed it would be the most merciful thing to do. Everyone was merely struggling to survive in the harsh realities of the world in which they have been born. The arrival of Islam and the teachings of the Quran put an end to all these.

Why are Muslim men allowed to marry up to four wives?

At this point, it must be made clear that the Quran *allows*, not *commands*, a man to have as much as four wives. Contrary to popular opinion, having multiple wives isn't some sort of pleasure spree. In Islam, it is the man who is responsible for providing for his wife. So taking more than one wife is not viewed as a means to multiply one's pleasure but to increase his responsibility.

Men are only allowed to take more than one wife *if* he is able to support *all* of them financially. Furthermore, he is required to treat them equally, to divide equally among them his time and his affection. He thus follows a rotating schedule for his visits. The same goes with his children from all women. He needs to provide them all with living accommodations, sustenance, education, leisure, etc.

It is necessary to understand that this kind of setup was developed as a way to provide solutions to the very real issues that people are facing. Such issues include poverty and the shortage of men. In certain situations, women would prefer to be a co-wife rather than not being anyone's wife at all.

In an era before Islam, if a man wanted a wife, he may *buy* as many women as he pleased. The 4 wives rule in the Quran served not as a license but as a *limitation* in the number of women men may marry.

Understand, too, that back in those days, war was frequent. And as mentioned, before Islam, there were no laws that protected females and children. Polygyny was Islam's effort to save widowed women, orphaned children, and females who had no means of livelihood. Note that before Islam, most Arab women were not given the right for education or employment. The only means for them to survive in such a harsh environment was for a man to take them under his wing.

Simply put, the taking of more than one wife is not a ticket to indulge in sexual pleasure. Rather, it is a challenge to take on bigger responsibilities to ensure the happiness, the health, and the security of women and children.

Still, isn't that unfair? Why aren't women allowed to marry more than one man?

Allah does not create rules without a purpose. If he believed that enabling a woman to marry more than one man would be for the good of all, then no doubt he would've allowed it. But the truth is there's purpose in doing so.

Furthermore, this setup is likely to create complex issues that would disturb the peace among his people. Firstly, there's the issue of inheritance. If a child has several fathers and one mother, it would be a challenge to determine who sired the child.

Moreover, in Islam, it is the man's obligation to provide for the whole family. If a woman is married to three husbands, this means that the three men's resources would go to her and her alone! That hardly fits into Allah's commandment of just distribution of goods and into Islam's goal of providing all women and children with a better life. Indeed, those two other men's resources (and affections) should have been allocated to other women, to other would-be children.

That said, one should know that these days, women in Islam are allowed to obtain employment and support themselves.

What does Islam say about terrorism?

Contrary to popular opinion, the God of Islam does not order his followers to kill others who do not share their faith. This misconception was brought about by the actions of Islam's extremists. Unfortunately, in all religions, there will always be radicals who misinterpret the message of their faith. The truth is that Islam explicitly forbids humans to take the life of another. That is, with the exception of self-defense, carrying out capital punishment for murder and when engaging in war.

According to the Quran, we are not allowed to take a life which Allah has made sacred.

The Quran *never* commanded followers to eradicate non-believers. However, some followers of the faith tend to misinterpret the verse which says that one must *fight non-believers* wherever one finds them.

This command was created *not* to urge the people to battle. Rather, this simply means that they should not run away from their oppressors. Because after all, a life of oppression is far worse than to die fighting for what is right. To put it plainly, when injustice occurs, followers of Islam are taught not to take it lying down. After all, we must prostrate ourselves only before God and not before man.

Muslims are allowed to fight their oppressors in the way of God. However, they are also reminded that Allah does not look kindly upon aggression.

Lastly, this is the frequently overlooked part of that verse in the Quran: If the oppressors stop being hostile, then one must remember the merciful and forgiving nature of Allah.

In conclusion, religion may reveal to us everything that is good and yet, in the end, it all lies in the interpretation and the actions of the follower.

Conclusion

Thank you again for downloading this book!

I hope this book was able to help you gain a deeper understanding of the Islam religion and its followers. With the shedding of several layers of misconceptions, I hope that you were able to see and appreciate the beauty and goodness of the Muslim way of life.

Finally, if you enjoyed this book, then I'd like to ask you for a favor, would you be kind enough to leave a review for this book on Amazon? It'd be greatly appreciated!

Click here to leave a review for this book on Amazon!

Thank you and I wish you a lifetime of peace and contentment as your soul finds its way back to Allah. ☺

Made in the USA
Middletown, DE
08 December 2017